ScottForesman

D'Nealian® Handwriting

Third Edition

Book **2**

Author
Donald Neal Thurber

ScottForesman

A Division of HarperCollinsPublishers

Editorial Offices: Glenview, Illinois
Regional Offices: Sunnyvale, California • Tucker, Georgia
Glenview, Illinois • Oakland, New Jersey • Dallas, Texas

Acknowledgments

Text
Page 51: From *The Mother's Day Sandwich*. Text copyright © 1990 by Jillian Wynot. Illustrations copyright © 1990 by Maxie Chambliss. Reprinted with permission of the publisher, Orchard Books, a division of Franklin Watts, Inc.
Page 125: Reprinted with permission of Four Winds Press, an Imprint of Macmillan Publishing Company from *Dinosaurs, Dragonflies & Diamonds: All About Natural History Museums* by Gail Gibbons. Copyright © 1988 by Gail Gibbons.

Illustrations
Laura D'Argo 19, 27, 50, 81, 92; Dawn DeRosa 64, 65, 68, 76, 90, 115, 116, 117, 119; Judith Love 25, 44, 45; Lane Gregory 105, 106, 110; Yoshi Miyake 20, 42, 43; Deborah Morse 100, 101; Jan Palmer 23, 28; Gary Phillips 118; Gail Roth 82; Judy Sakaguchi 58, 75, 89, 111, 123; Jeff Severn 8, 54, 60; Lena Shiffman 30, 31, 32, 33, 34, 35, 37, 39, 40, 97, 98; Georgia Shola 9, 10; Susan Swan 86, 87; Titus Tomescu 18; Jenny Vainsi 67, 94; Joe Veno 69, 91; Darcy Whitehead 3, 4, 5, 11, 29, 49, 59, 84, 85, 93, 102, 103; Jeannie Winston 95

Photographs
H. Armstrong Roberts 72, 73; Photo Researchers/P. B. Kaplan 71 (top); Superstock, Inc. 71 (center); Tony Stone Worldwide 63, 83

Staff Credits
Editorial: Marianne Hiland, Gerry Murphy-Ferguson, Delores Nemo, and Judith Nelson
Design: Paula Meyers
Production: Barbara Albright and Maryann Lewis
Marketing: Sue Cowden and Kristine Stanczak

D'Nealian® Handwriting is a registered trademark of Donald Neal Thurber.

ISBN: 0-673-28531-6
Copyright © 1993
Scott, Foresman and Company, Glenview, Illinois
All Rights Reserved. Printed in the United States of America.

16 17 18 19 20 21 22 -WC- 02 01 00 99

Contents

4

Unit One
Getting Ready to Write

Left-handed Position for Writing

Sit tall.
Put both feet on the floor.

Slant your paper as shown in the picture.
Hold it with your right hand.

Hold your pencil lightly between
your fingers. Study the picture.

Right-handed Position for Writing

Sit tall. Put both feet on the floor.

Slant your paper as shown in the picture. Hold it with your left hand.

Hold your pencil lightly between your fingers. Study the picture.

Letter Size and Form

a c e i m n o r s u v w x z

b d f h k l t   *g j p q y*

Manuscript letters have only three sizes. There are small letters, tall letters, and letters with descenders.

Small letters sit on the bottom line. They touch the middle line. Write three small letters.

Tall letters also sit on the bottom line. They touch the top line. Write three tall letters.

Descend means "go down." Letters with descenders have tails that go down under the bottom line. The descenders touch the line below. Write three letters with descenders.

Forming letters correctly helps make handwriting easy to read. Some letters, like **a** and **b,** must be closed. The letters **t** and **f** must be crossed. Dot the letters **i** and **j.**

Can you read the word below?

gift

The word is **gift.** Why is it so hard to read? What did the writer forget to do?

Write the word **gift** correctly. Close the letter **g.** Dot the **i.** Cross the **f** and the **t.**

Is your word easier to read?

8

Trace and write the sentences.
Remember the apostrophes. [']
A sentence that shows strong feeling
ends with an exclamation mark. [!]

Let's be careful!

Let's be careful!

Follow traffic signals.

Follow traffic signals.

Barb's bicycle has a bell and a flag.

*Barb's bicycle has a bell
and a flag.*

Writing Manuscript tT, hH, and kK

Trace and write the letters.

t	t	t
T	T	T
h	h	h
H	H	H
k	k	k
K	K	K

24

Writing Directions

Taylor will ride his bike to his friend Leon's house after school. Leon gave Taylor directions. Leon's directions are neatly written. Taylor can read them easily.

Copy Leon's directions. Make sure your letters are evenly spaced. Leave more space between words than between letters in a word.

Bell Lane

King School

Fifth Street

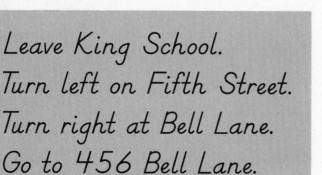

Leave King School.
Turn left on Fifth Street.
Turn right at Bell Lane.
Go to 456 Bell Lane.

Writing Manuscript iI and uU

Trace and write the letters.

Trace and write the sentences.
Remember that the pronoun **I** is always capitalized.

I will play a unicorn.

I will play a unicorn.

Invite your family and your friends.

Invite your family and your friends.

Up goes the curtain!

Up goes the curtain!

Writing Manuscript wW and yY

Trace and write the letters.

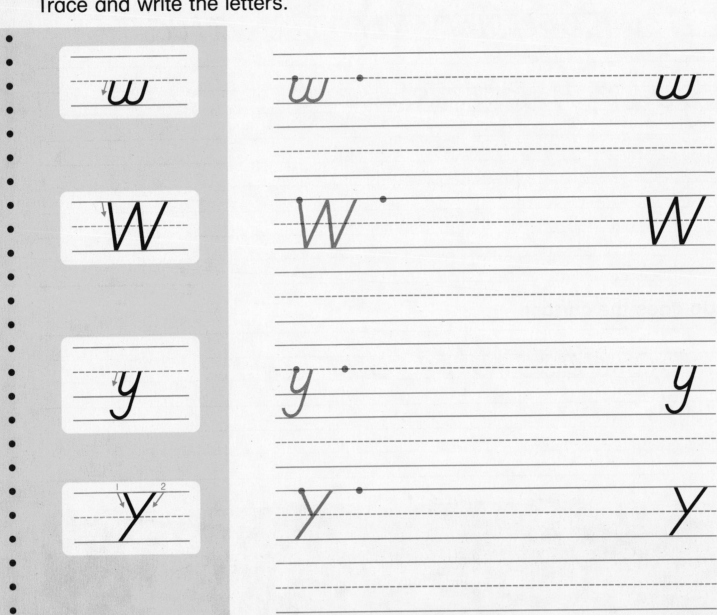

Trace and write the sentences.

We worked on Wednesday.

We worked on Wednesday.

Wendy drew a yellow sun.

Wendy drew a yellow sun.

Yoshi drew windows.

Yoshi drew windows.

We were very busy.

We were very busy.

Writing Manuscript jJ and rR

Trace and write the letters.

Talent Show

34

Cursive Is Coming

Sarah's class makes lists of what is served in the school lunchroom every day.

Sarah and her teacher wrote their lists in different ways. Most of the letters are joined in Mrs. Stone's list.

One place where letters are joined has been marked for you. Mark two more places where letters are joined.

Manuscript
You already know how to write like this.

Cursive
You will soon learn how to write like this.

Lunchroom Menu

Name *Sarah*

Day *Friday*

pizza

salad

fruit cup

milk

Lunchroom Menu

Name *Mrs. Stone*

Day *Friday*

pizza

salad

fruit cup

milk

41

Writing Manuscript qQ and vV

Trace and write the letters.

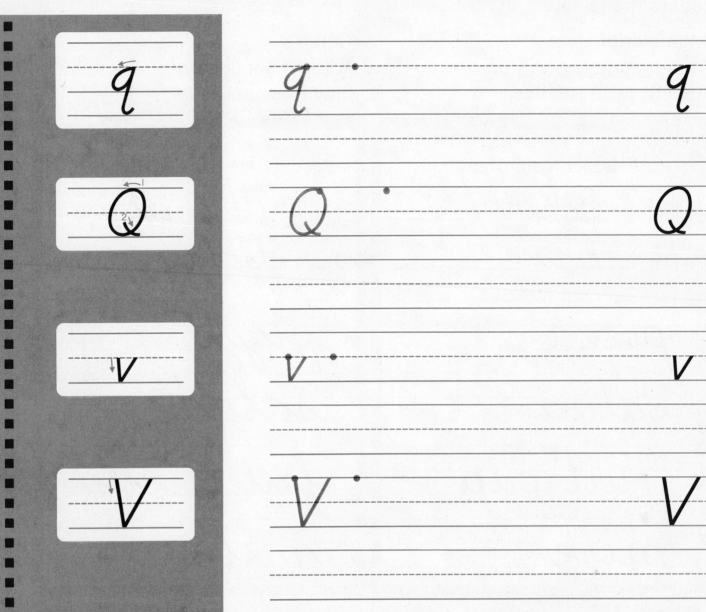

Trace and write the sentences.

Quinn bought seven quarts of milk.

Quinn bought seven quarts of milk.

Vic is quite lucky to have five quarters.

Vic is quite lucky to have five quarters.

Vi shops very quickly.

Vi shops very quickly.

Writing Manuscript zZ and xX

Trace and write the letters.

z   z

Z   Z

x   x

X   X

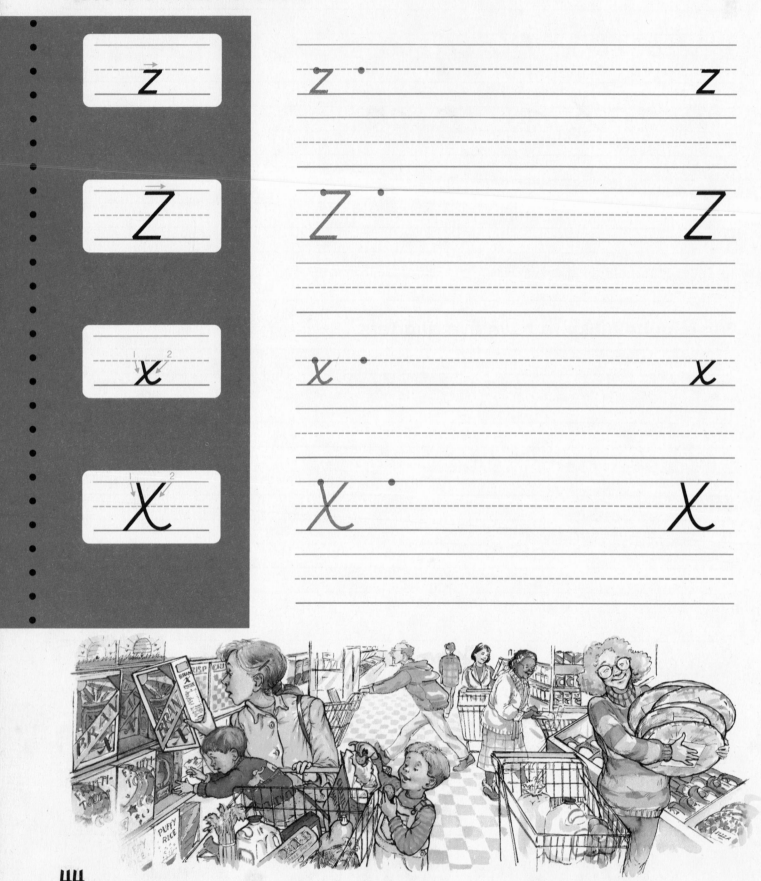

Review

Write the words.

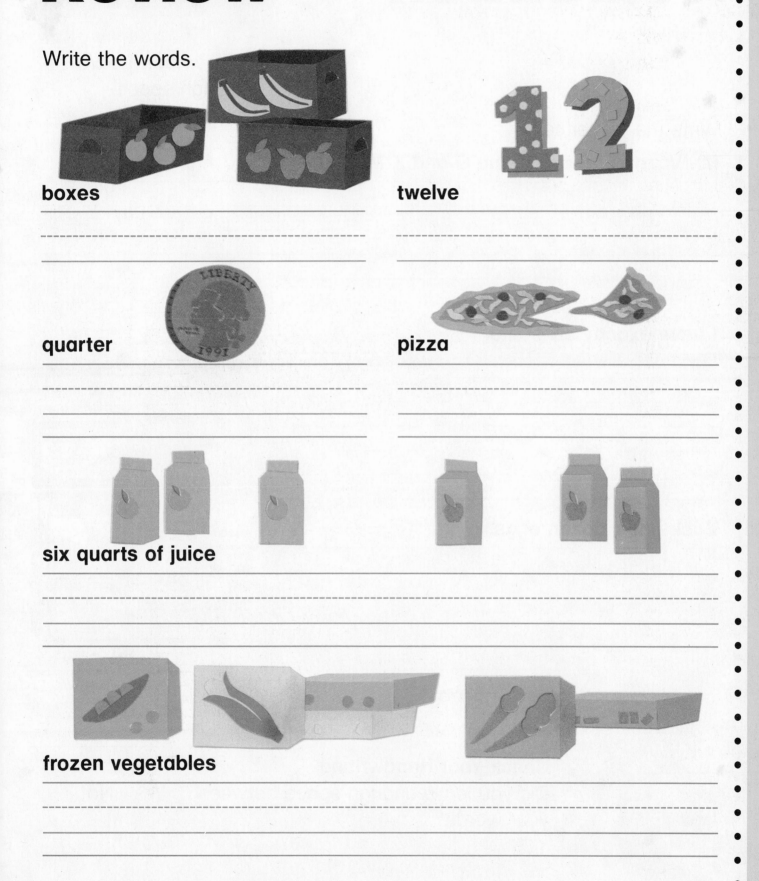

boxes

twelve

quarter

pizza

six quarts of juice

frozen vegetables

Evaluation

Remember: Leave enough space between words.

Write the sentences.

Mr. Vazquez drove to the Q and X Market.

I have exactly six cents.

Zack got a dozen eggs.

Check Your Handwriting
Did you leave enough space between your words?

Yes ☐   No ☐

Reading and Writing

In the book *The Mother's Day Sandwich* by Jillian Wynot, Hackett and Ivy made a surprise breakfast for their mother. All the food spilled and their surprise flopped.

Read this part of the story to find out what Mama did to make Hackett and Ivy feel better.

Mama pulled them back. "You don't make a Mother's Day sandwich in the kitchen. You can make it right here."

"Here?" said Ivy.

"Yes," said Mama. "You be one slice of bread, Ivy. And Hackett, you be the other slice. And I will be the cheese."

Hackett and Ivy giggled.

"Now, listen, you two pieces of bread," said Mama. "Squeeze very close to the cheese, so it can't fall out."

Ivy and Hackett squeezed very close to the cheese.

"Happy Mother's Day," said the two slices of bread.

"Thank you," said the cheese.

Think about a surprise sandwich you might make for someone special. Write some words in the Word Bank below to help you tell about this sandwich.

Word Bank

_____   _____
- - - - - - - - - - - - - - -   - - - - - - - - - - - - - - -
_____   _____
- - - - - - - - - - - - - - -   - - - - - - - - - - - - - - -
_____   _____
- - - - - - - - - - - - - - -   - - - - - - - - - - - - - - -
_____   _____

...istin decided to write about a surprise sandwich. Read the sentence she wrote to start her story.

I would make a pretty sandwich of tiny stars cut out of baloney.

Look at what Kristin wrote.

	Yes	No
• Did she use describing words to tell about her surprise sandwich?	☐	☐
• Can you picture the sandwich Kristin would make?	☐	☐

Look at how Kristin wrote it.

	Yes	No
• Do all her small letters touch the middle line?	☐	☐
• Do all her tall letters touch the top line?	☐	☐
• Do all her descenders touch the line below?	☐	☐

Circle any letters that are not the correct size.

Now it's your turn to write. Describe a surprise sandwich you might make for someone special. You may want to use the words from your Word Bank.

_____

- -

_____

- -

_____

- -

_____

- -

_____

- -

_____

- -

_____

Look at what you wrote.   Yes   No
- Did you use any describing words to tell about
  your surprise sandwich?   ☐   ☐
- Would a person reading about your sandwich be
  able to picture it?   ☐   ☐

Look at how you wrote it.
- Do your small letters touch the middle line?   ☐   ☐
- Do your tall letters touch the top line?   ☐   ☐
- Do your descenders touch the line below?   ☐   ☐

Make any changes that are needed. Then
make a clean copy on another sheet of paper.

Welcome to the Cursive Club!

The words above are in cursive. Members of the Cursive Club can read and write in cursive. What does cursive look like to you?

cooked spaghetti?	a secret code?	letters you already know?
		Do you know cursive?

You're right if you said cursive looks like letters you already know. Look at each letter in the messages below. Circle the cursive letters that look almost the same as manuscript letters.

We can't wait for cursive!

We can't wait for cursive!

Most cursive letters are joined together. Make a ⌣ under five places where letters are joined.

Congratulations! You are learning cursive. Soon you will be a member of the Cursive Club!

Strokes That Make Cursive Letters

To write cursive **l, h, k, t, i, u,** and **e,** add **uphill strokes** to the letters you already know. These letters already have ending strokes. To write cursive **j** and **p,** begin with an uphill stroke and add an ending stroke.

With your finger, trace the red uphill stroke in each letter. Circle the ending stroke in each letter.

uphill strokes

Uphill strokes can be tall or short. Practice each one.

To write a word in cursive, join the ending stroke in one letter with the beginning stroke in the next letter.

The letters **k, i, t,** and **e** begin with uphill strokes. Ending strokes and uphill strokes are joined in the word **kite.** Trace the word.

55

To write cursive **a, d, c, n, m,** and **x,** add **overhill strokes** to the letters you already know. These letters already have ending strokes. To write cursive **g, y,** and **q,** begin with an overhill stroke and add an ending stroke.

With your finger, trace the red overhill stroke in each letter. Circle the ending stroke in each letter.

overhill stroke

a d c n m x   g y q

Practice the overhill stroke.

The letters **m, a, n,** and **y** begin with overhill strokes. Ending strokes and overhill strokes are joined in the word **many.** Trace the word.

m a n y   many

The cursive letters **o, w,** and **b** end with a **sidestroke.**

With your finger, trace the red sidestroke in each letter.

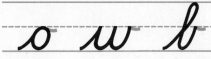

Practice the sidestroke.

A letter with a sidestroke must join the following letter near the middle line. This changes the beginning stroke of the following letter. Notice how the sidestroke changes **n, y,** and **e** in the words below. Trace the words.

sidestroke

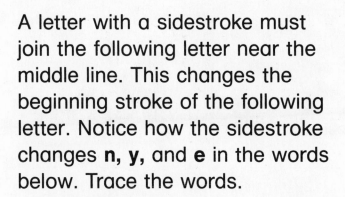

Most cursive letters look like the manuscript letters you already know. The letters **v, z, s, r,** and **f** look different.

Circle the uphill letters. Underline the overhill letters. Put a ✔ above the sidestroke letter.

v ν   z ʒ   s s   r ɾ   f f

Reading Cursive

Three messages are in the Cursive Clubhouse.
The writer has torn the messages in half.
Draw a line from the beginning of each
message to its missing part.

Cursive Club

The party   *a friend.*

It's at the   *is today.*

Bring   *clubhouse.*

58

Name

Unit Three
Writing Lower-case Cursive Letters

Letter Size and Form

Cursive letters come in the same three sizes as manuscript letters. There are small letters, tall letters, and letters with descenders.

Trace these small letters.

Trace these tall letters.

Trace these letters with descenders.

 *e i*

 *l t*

 *j q*

You want people to be able to read what you have written. To make your handwriting easy to read, be sure to form your letters correctly. Here are some things to remember about forming cursive letters.

Some cursive letters must be closed.

Some cursive letters have loops.

You must retrace when you write some cursive letters.

a o s

f g k

d n t

Look at the cursive alphabet below. Circle four letters that must be closed. Underline five letters that have loops. Put a ✔ above three letters that have retracing.

a b c d e f g h i j

k l m n o p q r

s t u v w x y z

Writing Cursive y and q

You can see manuscript **y** and **q** in cursive **y** and **q**. Begin with an overhill stroke. Add an ending stroke. Trace and write the letters.

Trace and write the words.

quite tiny

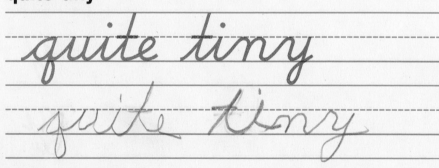

play quietly

73

a

d

c c

n n

m m

x x

g g

y y

q q

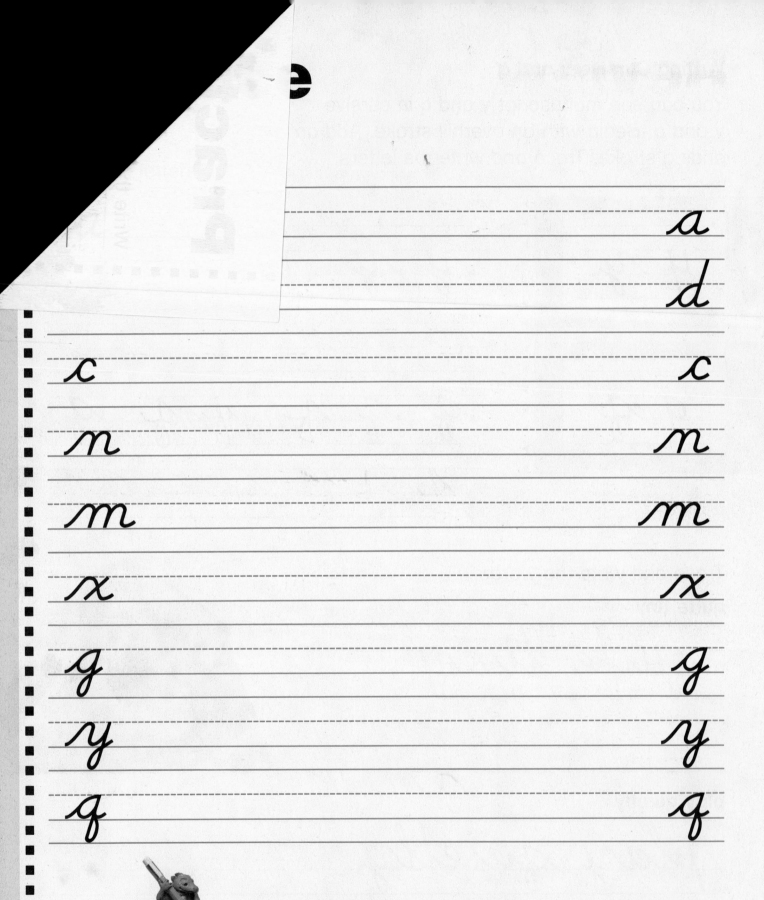

Circle your best letter in each line.

$\textcircled{a}$

Review

Write the words.

panda

cage

exit

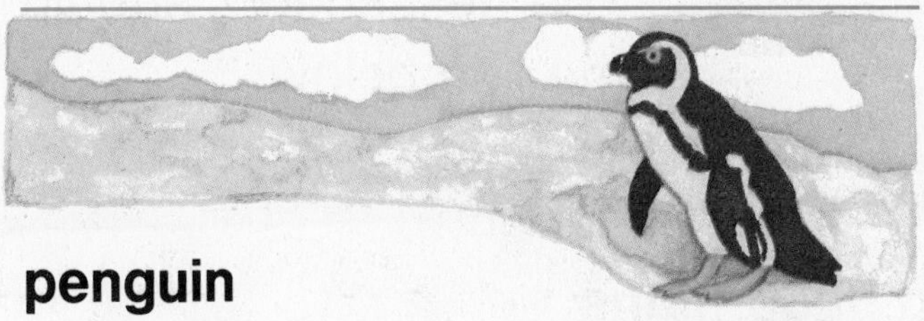

penguin

a quick chimp

a chilly animal

Evaluation

Remember: The letters **g**, **y**, and **q** have descenders. The descenders should touch the line below.

Write the words.

a huge mane

_____

- -

_____

_____

a quacking duck

_____

- -

_____

_____

my exciting day

_____

- -

_____

_____

Check Your Handwriting   Yes   No
Do your descenders touch the line below?   ☐   ☐

76

Letter Slant and Spacing

When you write in cursive, slant all your letters the same way. You may slant your letters to the right or to the left. You may write them straight up and down. Do not slant your letters in different ways.

right   *left*

up and down   *different*

Which writing is hard to read? Why is it hard?

Use correct spacing when you write. The letters in a word should be evenly spaced. Leave more space between words than between letters in a word.

ahugecat   *a huge cat*

Which writing is easier to read? Why is it easier?

Write these words. Slant all your letters the same way. Use correct spacing.

hidden in the jungle

	Yes	No
Do all your letters slant the same way?	☐	☐
Are the letters in your words evenly spaced?	☐	☐
Did you leave enough space between the words?	☐	☐

Writing Cursive o and w

You can see manuscript **o** and **w** in cursive **o** and **w.** Begin cursive **o** with an overhill stroke. Begin cursive **w** with an uphill stroke. Both letters end with a sidestroke. Trace and write the letters.

o o
w w

Cursive **o** and **w** join the next letter near the middle line. This changes the beginning stroke of the next letter. Trace and write the words.

a yellow yoyo

a yellow yoyo

a new wagon

a new wagon

Writing Cursive b

Cursive **b** looks a little like manuscript **b.**
Begin with an uphill stroke and end with a
sidestroke. Trace and write the letter.

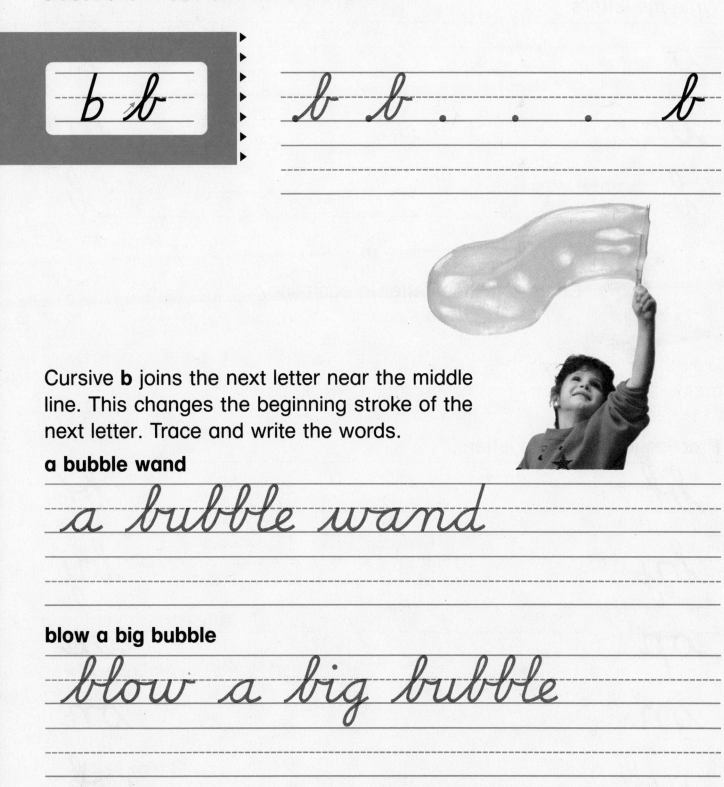

Cursive **b** joins the next letter near the middle
line. This changes the beginning stroke of the
next letter. Trace and write the words.

a bubble wand

a bubble wand

blow a big bubble

blow a big bubble

79

Practice

Write the letters.

o		o
w		w
b		b

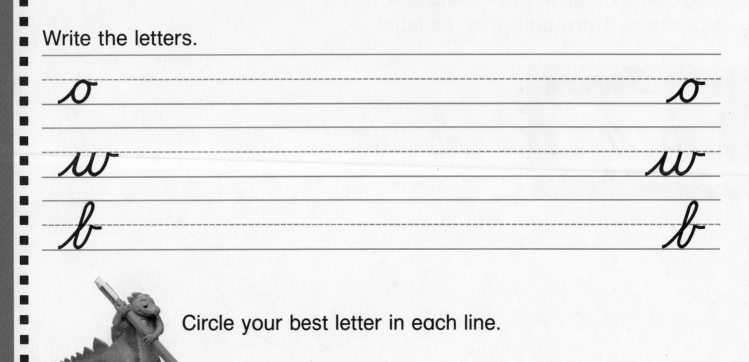

Circle your best letter in each line.

Practice joining these letters.

bl		bl
by		by
op		op
on		on
wh		wh

Review

Write the words.

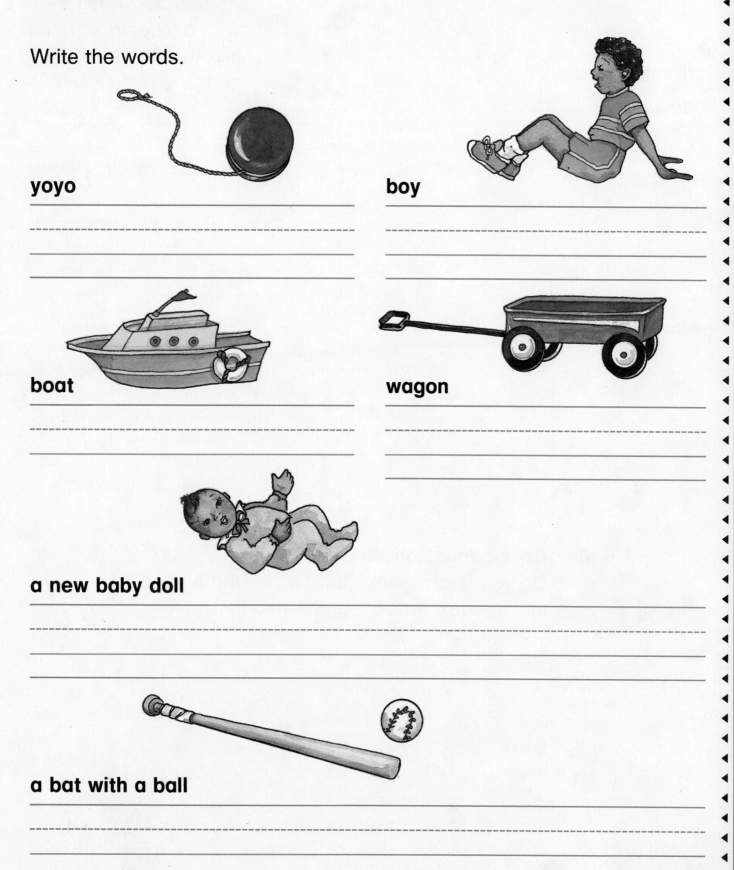

yoyo

boy

boat

wagon

a new baby doll

a bat with a ball

81

Evaluation

Remember: A letter with a sidestroke must join the next letter near the middle line.

Write the words.

one wooden block

my own cowboy hat

a book about a bug and a bug box

Check Your Handwriting
Do your sidestroke letters **o, w,** and **b** each join the next letter near the middle line?

Yes   No

82

Writing Cursive v and z

Cursive **v** and **z** do not look like manuscript **v** and **z**. Begin cursive **v** and **z** with an overhill stroke. Cursive **v** ends with a sidestroke. Trace and write the letters.

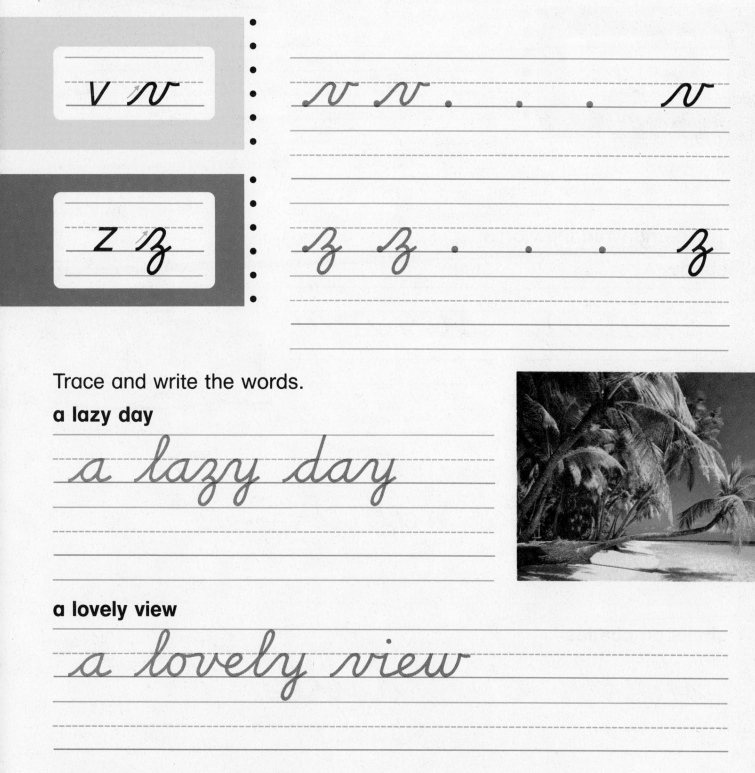

Trace and write the words.

a lazy day

a lazy day

a lovely view

a lovely view

Writing Cursive s

Cursive **s** does not look like manuscript **s.**
Begin cursive **s** with an uphill stroke. Trace
and write the letter.

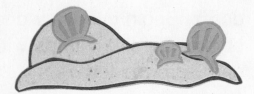

s s .   .   . s

Trace and write the words.

sandy

sandy

sunny

sunny

sea and sand

sea and sand

shells on castles

shells on castles

84

Writing Cursive r

Cursive **r** does not look like manuscript **r**.
Begin cursive **r** with an uphill stroke. Trace
and write the letter.

r r

r   r   .   .   .   r

Trace and write the words.

under the water

under the water

three large crabs in a hurry

*three large crabs in a
hurry*

Writing Cursive f

Cursive **f** does not look like manuscript **f**.
Begin cursive **f** with an uphill stroke. Trace
and write the letter.

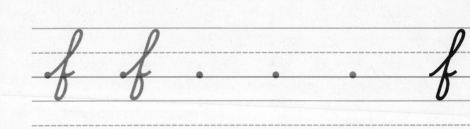

Trace and write the words.

fancy fins on fish

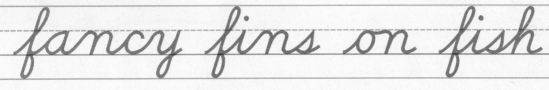

fancy fins on fish

five different fish

five different fish

86

Joining Sidestroke Letters

The letters **o, w, b,** and **v** must join the next letter near the middle line. This changes the beginning stroke of the next letter. Trace and write the joined letters and words.

ve ve ve

dive

br br br

brave

or or or

shore

os os os

toss

ws ws ws

claws

Practice

Write the letters.

v   v

z   z

s   s

r   r

f   f

Circle your best letter in each line.

(v)

Practice joining these letters.

fr   shr

vy   zz

Review

Write the words.

shovel

_____

_____

waves

_____

_____

starfish

_____

_____

shark

_____

_____

a dozen shells

_____

_____

very fluffy towels

_____

_____

Evaluation

Remember: Small letters should touch the middle line.

Write the words.

your first dive

fish zigzagging past

my favorite seashell

Check Your Handwriting
Do your small letters touch the middle line?

Yes   No
☐   ☐

Letter Size, Form, Slant, and Spacing

Write the words in your best cursive handwriting.

Form your letters correctly.

as red as a lobster

Did you form your letters correctly?   Yes ☐   No ☐

Make your letters the right height.

as slippery as an eel

Did you make your letters the right height?   Yes ☐   No ☐

Slant all your letters the same way.

like a fish out of water

Did you slant all your letters the same way?   Yes ☐   No ☐

Use correct letter and word spacing.

as happy as a clam

Did you use correct letter and word spacing?   Yes ☐   No ☐

Writing a List

The Parks family planned a trip to the beach. Mrs. Parks made a list of things to bring. Copy her list on the lines below. Plan your writing so that each thing on the list fits on one line.

two old blankets
five towels
a beach umbrella
sunscreen
pails and shovels
juice and popcorn
cups and napkins

Name

Unit Four
Writing Capital Cursive Letters

Writing Cursive A and C

Cursive **A** does not look like manuscript **A**.
Cursive **C** looks like manuscript **C**.
Trace and write the letters.

Trace and write the sentence. Be sure to join
cursive **A** and **C** to the letter that comes next.

Come to the amazing Apollo Circus!

*Come to the amazing
Apollo Circus!*

Writing Cursive E and O

Cursive **E** looks a little like manuscript **E**.
You can see manuscript **O** in cursive **O**.
Trace and write the letters.

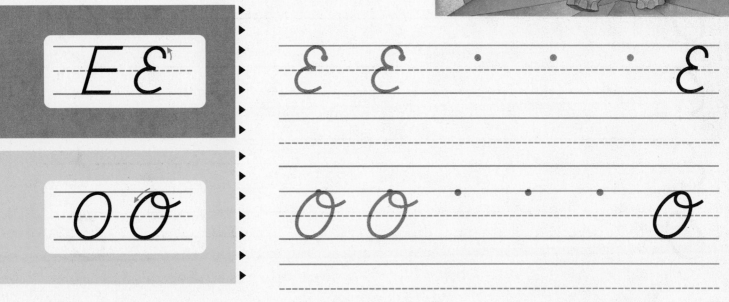

Trace and write the sentences.
Join cursive **E** to the letter that follows it.
Do not join cursive **O** to the next letter.

Elephants take a bow.

Elephants take a bow.

Omar trains them.

Omar trains them.

Practice

Write the letters.

a   *a*

C   *C*

E   *E*

O   *O*

Circle your best letter in each line.

a

Write the names.

Ollie's Clown Company

Eva's Acrobats

Annie's Animals

Review

Write the words and sentences from the signs.

Entrance
_____
- - - - - - - - - - - - - -
_____

Exit
_____
- - - - - - - - - - - - - -
_____

Otto
_____
- - - - - - - - - - - - - -
_____
_____

Ajax
_____
- - - - - - - - - - - - - -
_____
_____

Come One! Come All!
_____
- - - - - - - - - - - - - -
_____

Evaluation

Remember: Capital **A**, **C**, and **E** should be joined to the letters that follow them.

Write the sentences.

Everyone enjoys Elmo.

_____

_____

Coco the clown went to Clown College.

_____

_____

Once Al saw a circus.

_____

_____

Check Your Handwriting
Do your capital **A**, **C**, and **E** join the letters that follow them?

Yes   No

☐   ☐

98

Addressing an Envelope

Carla wrote to her pen pal, Andrew, to tell him about the circus. Then she addressed an envelope for her letter.

Copy the addresses in the space below. Form your letters and numbers correctly so the Postal Service will know where to deliver the letter. Try to keep your writing straight even though there are no writing lines. Notice that the addresses are written in capital manuscript letters.

CARLA CRUZ
605 ELM AVENUE
OAKLAND CA 94610

ANDREW EVANS
77 OAK COURT
ORLANDO FL 32804

Writing Cursive H and K

You can see manuscript **H** and **K** in cursive **H** and **K**. Trace and write the letters.

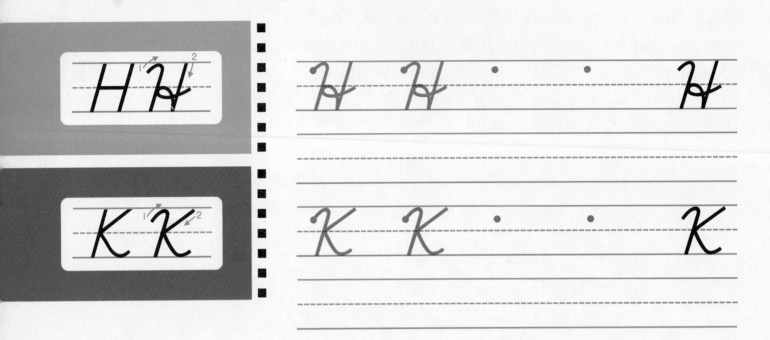

Trace and write the sentence.
Join cursive **K** to the letter that follows it.
Do not join cursive **H** to the next letter.

Kathy Hobbs works at Kane Hospital.

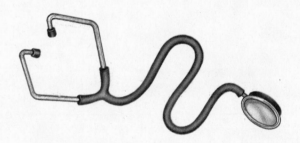

Kathy Hobbs works at
Kane Hospital.

Writing Cursive N and M

Cursive **N** and **M** look a little like manuscript **N** and **M**. Trace and write the letters.

Nn   *n   n • • n*

Mm   *m   m • • m*

Trace and write the sentence. Join cursive **N** and **M** to the letters that follow them.

Mr. Nash plays in the Melody Makers.

Mr. Nash plays in the

Melody Makers.

Writing Cursive U and V

Cursive **U** looks very much like manuscript **U**.
Cursive **V** looks a little like manuscript **V**.
Trace and write the letters.

Trace and write the sentence.
Join cursive **U** to the letter that follows it.
Do not join cursive **V** to the next letter.

Uncle Vic is a waiter at the Village Cafe.

Uncle Vic is a waiter at the Village Cafe.

Writing Cursive W and Y

Cursive **W** and **Y** look a little like manuscript **W** and **Y**. Trace and write the letters.

$\mathcal{W}$ $\mathcal{W}$ · · $\mathcal{W}$

$\mathcal{Y}$ $\mathcal{Y}$ · · $\mathcal{Y}$

Trace and write the sentence.
Join cursive **Y** to the letter that follows it.
Do not join cursive **W** to the next letter.

Yes, Yolanda works for World Airlines.

Yes, Yolanda works for World Airlines.

Practice

Write the letters.

H   H

K   K

n   n

m   m

u   u

v   v

w   w

y   y

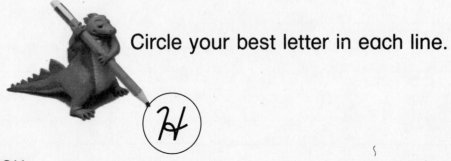

Circle your best letter in each line.

104

Review

Mr. Chandler's class wrote about their parents' jobs. Write the names of the places where some of the parents work. Remember to underline the titles of magazines, newspapers, and books.

Uptown Moving Vans

Wildlife Magazine

Ned's Animal Hospital

Yvette's Kitchen

Evaluation

Remember: All letters should rest on the bottom line.

Write the sentences.

Mayor Karl Utley works at City Hall.

_____
- -
_____
_____
- -
_____
_____

Vicky Young reports for the <u>Weekly News.</u>

_____
- -
_____
_____
- -
_____
_____

Check Your Handwriting
Do all your letters rest on the bottom line?

Yes ☐ No ☐

Writing Proper Nouns

Special names for people, places, and things are called proper nouns. Proper nouns begin with capital letters. Write these proper nouns. Use cursive handwriting.

Miss Helen Ko

65 East Villa Avenue

Omaha, Nebraska

North America

Wednesday

November 21

Charlie Needs a Cloak

Writing Cursive T and F

Cursive **T** and **F** look a little like manuscript **T** and **F**. Trace and write the letters.

Trace and write the sentence. Do not join cursive **T** and **F** to the letters that follow them.

Fred will go to Tim's party on Friday.

Fred will go to Tim's party on Friday.

Writing Cursive B

Cursive **B** looks like manuscript **B.** Trace and write the letter.

B B

B   B   B

Trace and write the sentences. Do not join cursive **B** to the letter that follows it.

Birthdays are fun.

Birthdays are fun.

Becky gave Bonnie a birthday gift.

Becky gave Bonnie a birthday gift.

Writing Cursive P and R

You can see manuscript **P** and **R** in cursive **P** and **R**. Trace and write the letters.

P P

P P P

R R

R R R

Trace and write the sentences.
Join cursive **R** to the letter that follows it.
Do not join cursive **P** to the next letter.

Paul opens the door.

Paul opens the door.

Please come in, Rita.

Please come in, Rita.

110

Choose the most interesting thing from the list you made on page 126. Write about it. Tell why you would like to see it.

_____

_____

_____

_____

_____

_____

_____

_____

_____

_____

_____

_____

_____

_____

_____

Look at what you wrote.   Yes   No
- Did you tell what you would like to see?   ☐   ☐
- Did you tell why you would like to see it?   ☐   ☐

Look at how you wrote it.
- Are all your letters slanted the same way?   ☐   ☐
- Is there enough space between your words?   ☐   ☐

Make any changes that are needed. Then make a clean copy on another sheet of paper.

Index